# THE BiG of Calmers

## Jenny Mosley and Ross Grogan

Positive Press

Published in 2009 by:
Positive Press Ltd
28A Gloucester Road
Trowbridge
Wiltshire BA14 0AA

Telephone: 01225 719204
Fax: 01225 712187
E-mail: positivepress@jennymosley.co.uk
Website: www.circle-time.co.uk

Text © Jenny Mosley and Ross Grogan
Re-printed 2010, 2011, 2012, 2013, 2015
ISBN 9-781904-866268

Illustrator: Mark Cripps

Printed in the U.K. Heron Press, www.heronpress.co.uk

# Contents:

# What are Calmers?

You will all be familiar with classroom moments when you feel the atmosphere becoming charged with negative energy. We experience these moments when children are overexcited or anxious and the bad feeling seems to catch on until everyone is restless and you know that you urgently need to find a way to settle them down and get them working calmly again. The big book of Calmers is a toolbox of activities which you can use with individuals, groups or a whole class to relieve stress and tension, or even as a quick pick-me-up. Many of them you can use yourself, whenever you feel your own stress levels rising.

# How can Calmers help?

A calm classroom has an ethos in which children feel more secure and can concentrate on their work. A calm classroom is, therefore, likely to be a happy classroom and a productive one, where children experience a sense of well-being. Calmers are designed to turn around negative thinking and build children's self-esteem. They promote emotional self-awareness, teach anger management, and improve children's ability to interact positively with each other.

Learning is hard work and, sometimes, it can be taxing and challenging. Children often express anxiety in physical ways and their tension becomes visible. You know when this is happening because they start to fidget and disrupt other children. They can also become emotional and get upset or angry or withdraw into themselves and refuse to interact in their usual ways. When you notice these behaviours starting to take over your setting, you need to do something quickly so that everyone gets a chance to calm down and settle themselves back on task. You can do this by offering a complete change of scene that helps them to forget about whatever it was that was making them overwrought. In other words, you need to give everyone a break: a time of relaxation or positivity that calms everyone down but doesn't take too long or interfere with your timetable.

It is worth noting that The Energizers book works in a similar way by orchestrating a mental change of direction. With Calmers, children are being redirected away from anxiety or over-excitement and towards calm alertness, where as with Energizers children are being redirected away from listlessness and into focused alertness. In other words, the same result is achieved but the starting points are very different. This is why, sometimes, Energizers and Calmers can appear similar.

# When can you use Calmers?

Calmers are quick: you can use them to start the day, end the day, to calm children down after a rowdy playtime, to steady their nerves before a test – in fact, at any time when the emotional temperature is rising. They can be fitted in at any time. They are not part of your direct teaching programme, although many of them can add an extra dimension to art, language work, or physical education. In particular, they will fit in well with Social and Emotional Aspects of Learning (SEAL). At the end of the day, you will all go home feeling far less tired and more fulfilled. However, when children need a boost of energy to wake them up we recommend you use an energizer from *The Big Book of Energizers.*

# Who can use Calmers?

Anyone who facilitates a group of learners can use Calmers. We have designed this book for use in primary and secondary schools. Some activities will suit younger children, some will suit older children. Many can be adapted for use in Early Years settings and for children with special educational needs. You can teach children to use some of these techniques independently, whenever they feel themselves getting anxious.

Weary staff and enthusiastic parents can benefit from Calmers too!

# What types of activities do we include in our Calmers?

A wide range of activities can be used to calm children down. Some activities calm children by calming their physical bodies, while others harness their imagination or calm them by changing negative thoughts into positive ones. Some activities set out to change the atmosphere of the whole room and others are suited for use with small groups or individuals. Activities include:

- stretches and relaxation techniques
- sensory stillness
- singing together
- music, rhythm and rhyme
- stories and poetry
- self-esteem boosters
- positive thinking

Each chapter of Calmers is grouped in a particular order. You will find them by the following symbols:

1. **Thumbs up** = activity can be played quickly and easily

2. **Index finger on the chin** = game will take a bit of organising by the teacher

3. **Pointing outside** = game will need a large space

## What type of activities do we include in our Calmers?

The activities are varied but we have been careful to include:

- basic relaxation techniques
- stretching
- controlled breathing
- guided visualisation
- imaginative activities
- positive thinking
- games to quieten stressed minds
- self-esteem boosters
- stories and songs
- drama and role play.

## Before you get started

Here are some useful points to think about before you start using Calmers:

- If you are asking children to make wide physical movements, do they have room to do so without knocking into each other?
- Do you know how to stop children from working or fidgeting and ask them to start your Calmer? It is best to work out a little routine like 'Hand Up' (see below).
- Have you thought what routine or signal you could use to stop the Calmers session and ask children to re-focus on their books, the board or your lesson? You need a quick and effective re-focusing routine to get back to the lesson.
- Do any of your pupils have special requirements that could make any of the activities difficult, embarrassing or awkward for them?
- For your first few times using Calmers, have you planned them really well, so that you don't have to focus on what to do and when but can focus on actually working with the children and benefiting from the activity?
- Have you got a list of Calmers to hand that you can use whenever you need them, with different themes to suit the mood of the class?
- Have you thought how to make the Calmers more helpful for the class? For example, by joining in yourself, by putting on music or incorporating lots of smiles?
- Will you use plenty of praise to compliment those who co-operate with each Calmer, listen well to you and do the activities well?
- Can you explain how to do the Calmers so that each child understands your expectations? Children will become frustrated if they do not understand what is expected.
- Will you be able to show the children your enthusiasm and happiness at having a productive break from the lesson? Let the children know it's a valuable thing to do – your conviction is infectious!
- It is vital to involve everyone, and experience tells us that giving some children the right to opt out and carry on working is likely to lead to other children doing this who may only pretend to be working while secretly hoping to cause a distraction. Try to be very resolute when you introduce the activity so that rebellious children don't have time to think of reasons not to join in.
- Encourage the children to drink plenty of water – a dehydrated brain does not work calmly.

- For activities that are challenging, it might be appropriate for a teaching assistant or other pupil to work in a pair with any pupil who has a learning disability, or has a limited understanding of English, to support their contribution.
- Brave schools know that staff need Calmers too! If your colleagues are coming into meetings looking stressed and drained, why not try out a few Calmers with them and see if they catch on.

All teachers need to train children to respond quickly and efficiently when the situation requires an instant response. We recommend that you use the following excellent technique whenever you do a Calmer.

### The Hand Up Approach to Silence

**Hold your arm up very straight and high.**
**Say NOTHING.**

**Stand very still and wait.**

**Children must respond by putting their hand up and touching**
**the shoulders of others who are talking – who then put their hands up.**

**Bring your hand down.**

**Say, 'Thank you'.**

**(Sometimes you can hold your hand up closed with a smiley-face**
**sticker hidden inside it and give this to the first child to respond,**
**and watch the ripple of attention!)**

# Physical Calmers

The activities in this section are designed to calm restless or anxious children by teaching them invaluable breathing and stretching techniques. Getting hot and bothered sets off many changes in our bodies – our heartbeat races, we become physically restless and feel uncomfortable and ill-at-ease, and stretching and body-control are effective ways to help children learn how to calm and relax themselves when they are tense, over-excited or anxious.

When we deal positively with the physical effects of stress and agitation, we quickly realize that our minds are calmed; our thoughts become steadier and we are able to regain control of our overexcited brains. Calm is restored.

All of the stretching and calming activities in this section are simple and easy to learn. No equipment is needed and many can be carried out in the classroom without the need to rearrange furniture or take time preparing space.

Once learned, children will be able to use them on their own whenever they feel the need to slow down and take a few moments to organize their thoughts and refresh their bodies.

# 1. Shoulder pull

*This calmer is a lovely spine stretcher.*

## What you need: nothing

## What to do:

Stand up straight.

Put both hands flat on the stomach, one on top of the other, and hold arms very stiff and straight.

Slowly raise the arms above the head.

Slowly lower them.

Change the hands over so that the one in front is now the one behind.

Repeat the lift.

# 2. Climb the ladder

*A whole-body calmer that rests the mind as well as the body.*

## What you need: nothing

## What to do:

Stand still with feet a shoulder-width apart.

Move arms and legs as if climbing a ladder up to the ceiling.

# 3. Lunges

*This calmer is a gentle, controlled stretch.*

## What you need: nothing

## What to do:

Stand with one foot in front of the other and both feet pointing straight ahead.

Lunge forward slowly. Do not bend the front knee too far. Stretch the back of the back leg.

Repeat with the other leg.

# 4. Tall as a tower

*This calmer loosens the spine and calms the emotions.*

## What you need: nothing

## What to do:

Stretch fingers up to the ceiling standing on tiptoes.

Hold for 10 seconds then relax.

Crouch down and hug knees.  Hold for a count of 10.

Return to standing position and stretch out arms as wide as possible.

Repeat.

# 5. Upper arm stretch

*This stretch warms the body and relaxes the neck.*

## What you need: nothing

## What to do:

Stand with feet shoulder-width apart.

Raise the right arm above the head and bend the elbow so that the hand rests on the back of the neck.

Now raise the left hand so that it rests on the right elbow.

Make a slight backward press to the elbow until you feel a gentle stretch in the right upper arm.

Hold the stretch for 10 seconds and repeat with the other arm.

# 6. A piece of string

*This calmer helps posture and breathing.*

## What you need: nothing

## What to do:

Teach your children to spend a few seconds standing very straight when they line up.

Ask them to imagine that a piece of string is attached to the top of their heads. Tell them that the string is pulling them up on to their tiptoes. This stills them, aligns their bodies, and fills their bodies with calming oxygen.

You can ask the group to stand at their table and do this stretch at any time of the day.

# 7. Handy calmer

*A simple calmer for any time of day.*

## What you need: nothing

## What to do:

When they are sitting, ask the children to rest the tips of the fingers and thumb of one hand gently against the tips of the fingers and thumb of the other hand. Then they must breathe slowly for one minute. This is wonderfully calming.

**Tip:** A good one for staff too.

# 8. Temple massage

*This is a simple but effective calmer.*

## What you need: nothing

## What to do:

Demonstrate how to gently massage the sides of their eyes and temples with soothing fingertips. Just move the fingers round and round in little circles – very relaxing.

**Tip:** Buy some scented oils and keep them in the staff room. Share them with colleagues on wearisome days and do the temple massage together.

# 9. Slow dancing

*This calmer requires concentration and unhurried movements to create lasting tranquillity in your setting.*

## What you need: nothing

## What to do:

Make slow, light movements with your arms and relax your expression. You could make slow mathematical shapes with your hands - like a circle and a square or a number eight.

Alternatively, ask everyone to become a room of slowly moving windmills for a little while. Ask them to move their arms round and round like a windmill on a slow, sunny day – this gives a good stretch and relaxes everyone too.

**Tip:** When you feel stressed, try not to rush around.

# 10. Long-distance looking

*This calmer proves that, when our eyes are relaxed, the rest of our body quickly de-stresses.*

## What you need: nothing

## What to do:

Explain that eyes are at their most relaxed when they look at things that are a long way away. Ask everyone to look out of the window for a moment and see how far they can see.

Then they can return to their work feeling refreshed and calm.

Turn this into a game of 'I-spy', which has an added rule that participants must choose things that are in the far distance.

**Tip:** You can try this yourself..

# 11. Fingertip to wrist

*Another 'do anywhere' calmer that is surprisingly effective.*

## What you need: nothing

## What to do:

Stroke the back of each hand.  Stroke lightly from the fingertips to the wrist.  Do this gently and your hands will soon feel warm and you will feel calmer.

Try the same thing with your feet.

# 12. Slow breathing

*Controlling the breath gives us an immediate sense of calm.*

## What you need: nothing

## What to do:

Show everyone how to spend a minute slowing their breathing. Ask them to sit quietly with their hands in their laps, palms upward and count slow breaths, in and out, in and out. The room will become instantly calm and quiet.

Try adding a positive thought and repeat it to yourself over and over as the breath goes in and out. Affirmatives like, 'I am happy and calm', or 'I always do my best', are worth a try but it is a good idea to make up your own. Affirmations are always made in the present tense and are always positive.

**Tip:** Another good one for teachers too.

# 13. Calming facial muscles

*If your face is calm, the rest of you will surely follow.*

## What you need: nothing

## What to do:

- When we are tense, our jaw gets rigid. Show everyone how they can relax themselves by pressing their tongue on the roof of their mouth, just above the front teeth.

- There is a special place on either side of the bridge of the nose. Rub it gently and feel all that tension drift away.

- Close your eyes very, very slowly. As your lids get lower, you will feel a sense of wonderful calm waft through your body.

- Raise your eyebrows. You will feel tension lift as they rise. You can make this even better by frowning a big worry frown before you raise your brows. Alternatively, you can ask everybody to join you by making a 'surprised' face. This also raises the eyebrows and makes your face feel relaxed.

# 14. Slowing the pulse

*Our heart rate increases and slows in proportion to our level of tension.*

## What you need: nothing

## What to do:

Put your fingers on your wrist and find your pulse. Repeat quietly, 'My pulse is steady and calm', and very soon you will realize that it has become exactly that!

**Tip:** Do this exercise at the end of playtime and everyone will walk back to class feeling calm and ready to learn.

# 15. Foot rub

*This calmer shows that a foot rub can relax the whole body.*

## What you need: nothing

## What to do:

Make a fist and rub the soles of your feet. Press hard and your feet will send calming messages to the rest of your body in no time at all.

# 16. Sixty-second siesta

*This is a great calmer if you feel that your children are becoming overly anxious or too boisterous.*

## What you need: nothing

## What to do:

When you feel that your children need a short rest, call out the words, Sixty-second siesta.

When they hear this command, every child must stop what they are doing, clear a space on their desk and put their heads on their hands as if they have fallen asleep.

Tell the children that they are deeply asleep and are not able to move at all and you do not want to see any movement or twitches.

When you feel that everyone is calm, speak gently and evenly, saying, *Open your eyes slowly, and quietly go back to your work, children.*

When you have played it a few times, your children will respond to the cue instruction and take a minute's break quickly and easily.

# 17. A minute's peace

*If some of your children are becoming too noisy or restless why not give everyone a minute of complete peace and quiet.*

## What you need: nothing

## What to do:

When you feel that your class is getting too noisy and you need to quieten them, clap your hands and call out, *One minute's peace.*

The children must stop what they are doing and stand up. (If you have a wall clock in your classroom, some of them may need to turn round so that nobody is facing towards it. Children who have watches are not allowed to look at them.)

When they think a minute has passed, they must sit down, very quietly, with their hands on their laps.

The child who sits down at exactly one minute is the winner.

When everyone is sitting quietly, the winner is announced and the lesson can resume in an atmosphere of greater calm.

# 18. Relaxing letters

*The instructions you give will involve one way of relaxing. Here are some suggestions but you will find many others in this book.*

## What you need: nothing

## What to do:

All the children sit in their seats or in the quiet corner.

- Call out a letter of the alphabet. Children who have that letter in their name must follow your instructions while the rest of the class sits quietly.

- Call the letter A. Everyone with an A in their name must roll their head slowly in a circle.

- Call the letter G. Everyone with a G in their name must tense and then relax their feet.

- Call the letter E. Everyone who has an E in their name must stand with both arms raised high, feet shoulder-width apart and knees slightly bent. Then they must wave their arms from side to side like a tree.

- Call the letter B. Everyone who has a B in their name must massage the sides of their eyes and temples with soothing fingertips. Tell them to move their fingers round and round in little circles.

Continue in this way until everyone seems calm and relaxed.

# 19. Amusing movement

*This calmer uses laughter to ease tension in the shoulders, arms, legs and head.*

## What you need: nothing

## What to do:

Ask the children to sit in their seats while you stand up.

Demonstrate a funny movement. You may like to challenge them not to laugh, which increases its likelihood. Show them an amusing movement. Try one from the following selection:

- Hold your upper arms in a horizontal position and flap your lower arms.

- Walk like a penguin.

- Call the letter G. Everyone with a G in their name must tense and then relax their feet.

- Call the letter E. Everyone who has an E in their name must stand with both arms raised high, feet shoulder-width apart and knees slightly bent. Then they must wave their arms from side to side like a tree.

- Call the letter B. Everyone who has a B in their name must massage the sides of their eyes and temples with soothing fingertips. Tell them to move their fingers round and round in little circles.

Continue in this way until everyone seems calm and relaxed.

# 20. Stop, flop, drop

*This calmer is a quick way to soothe body and mind.*

## What you need: nothing

## What to do:

Use the following script to talk your group through this relaxation technique:

**Stop** *what you are doing and sit very still.*
*Concentrate on your body.  Notice how it feels.*
*Curl up your toes until they feel tight and scrunched up.*
*Scrunch up your knees*
*Scrunch up your elbows.*
*Scrunch up your whole body until all of it feels tight and crinkly.*
**Flop** *your feet so that they feel loose and sleepy.*
*Relax your body until all of it feels loose and floppy.*
*Sit or lie still for a little while and let your thoughts* **drop** *out of your brain until it is empty and calm.*
*Now listen to the sounds around you and feel the air on your face and hands.  Feel yourself filling up with peace and quietness.*

# 21. Slow blow

*A controlled calming activity that only takes a few seconds.*

## What you need: nothing

## What to do:

Ask the group to stand and focus their attention on something in front of them – a picture, a corner of the whiteboard, light-switch, etc.

Ask them to take a very deep breath and hold it for a moment.

Then they must purse their lips so that they are very tight, and slowly, very slowly, send the air out in a steady hissing stream that makes a quiet sssss sound.
Repeat if necessary.

# 22. Dog pant

*A calming way to fill your brain with oxygen.*

## What you need: nothing

## What to do:

Ask the children if they have ever seen a dog pant.

Ask them to take a deep breath and then to open their mouths and allow their jaw to sag and their tongue to relax completely.

Now they must pant like a dog pants, encouraging their diaphragm and stomach muscles to go up and down.

Repeat until everyone's brain is filled with oxygen and they all feel calm.

# 23. Stretch up, stretch down

*This calmer is a stretch and breathing exercise.*

## What you need: nothing

## What to do:

Ask the children to find a space on their own and to stand with the feet shoulder-width apart.

Use this script to lead the group through the exercise.

*Bend your knees just a little bit.*

*Breathe in and stretch your arms high above your head.*

*Now, very slowly, bend forward and reach down towards your feet. Breathe out as you bend down.*

Repeat the exercise five times.

# 24. Rabbit breathing

*This calmer is a quick pick-me-up for everyone.*

## What you need: nothing

## What to do:

Use the following script to lead the group in this exercise.

>*Sit comfortably and make your neck and back as straight and long as you can.*

>*Tuck in your chin, open your mouth and let your jaw relax.*

>*Take four quick breaths through your nose.*

>*Twitch your nose like a rabbit.*

>*Breathe out through your mouth in a long, smooth sigh.*

Repeat four times.

**Tip:** Increase the number of inhalations and double the length of your exhalations.

# 25. Smile yourself calm

*This calmer works because smiling is a wonderful mood changer.*

## What you need: nothing

## What to do:

Ask the group to sit comfortably.

Lead everyone in taking a few deep breaths and ask them to notice their mood.
Now show them how to pull their lips into a huge exaggerated smile. (It doesn't matter that it is false.)

Hold the smile for three or four seconds.

Repeat.

**Tip:** If you do this whenever the group needs to line-up, you will find that they walk much more quietly and calmly!

# 26. Self-head-massage

*This calmer is a gentle way to soothe away worries.*

## What you need: nothing

## What to do:

Guide the group in the following sequence of movements.

*Gently sweep your hands over your face with eyes shut.*

*Stroke your hair.*

*Lightly tap your scalp.*

*Gently knead and then stroke your own shoulders.*

**Tip:** If children are sensible and mature, they can be encouraged to do this for one another.

# 27. Thumb massage

*Acupressure is a relaxing, self-help technique.*

## What you need: nothing

## What to do:

Demonstrate how you can press your right thumb over your left palm.

Show the group how you work round in circles, pressing and kneading as you go.

Explain that, if you find a place that is slightly tender or tense, you have found an area that needs extra work and keep pressing gently until the skin feels softer and less tense.

Let the group have a go at this safe, gentle, form of acupressure.

Join everyone in a good hand wiggle and shake.

**Tip:** Worth trying with children who hold their writing pens too tightly.

# 28. Sand-timer moment

*Extend concentration through practise.*

## What you need: nothing

## What to do:

Use a sand-timer to give children a period of calm.

Put the sand-timer where everyone can see it and ask the group to watch quietly as the sand moves through the glass.

Extend periods of sustained concentration for members of the group. Make them aware that you are doing this by informing them of the times involved. This helps them to feel the pleasure of knowing that they are maturing and becoming more focused and skilled.

# 29. Calm a tension headache

*This technique utilizes the power of acupressure.*

## What you need: nothing

## What to do:

Show the group the pressure point that is located between the eyebrows, in the indentation between the bridge of the nose and the forehead.

Encourage them to use their middle finger to apply gentle steady pressure on the point for one minute.

As the pressure is being applied, focus on slow, deep breathing.

Release the pressure after one minute, and tell the group to let their face muscles relax.

Repeat the exercise.

**Tip:** There will be days you will need this too!

# 30. Whole body de-stresser

*This is a great way to relax the whole body.*

## What you need: space to lie down

## What to do:

Everyone needs to lie down on the floor and make themselves comfortable.

Ask the children to clench the muscles in their toes and then relax them.

Now tighten the calf muscles, only to relax them a moment later.

Carry on up the body until it feels stress-free and relaxed.

**Tip:** This exercise can be done in the sitting position – even in the car or on the bus.

# 31. Stretch wide

*A calming stretch and breathing exercise to help everyone forget their anxieties.*

## What you need: space

## What to do:

Ask the children to find a space on their own and to stand with the feet shoulder-width apart.

Use this script to lead the group through the exercise.

> *Bend your arms and hold them up so that your hands are at shoulder height.*
>
> *Turn your palms so that they are facing outwards.*
>
> *Keep your body very still and push your palms outwards as if you are trying to push against two strong walls.*
>
> *Bring them back in towards your body again.*

Repeat this several times.

# 32. Just like a bird

*A gentle, calming stretch.*

## What you need: space

## What to do:

Ask the children to find a space on their own and to stand with the feet shoulder-width apart.

Use this script to lead the group through the exercise.

> *Bend your knees slightly and sink down a little.*
>
> *Breathe in.*
>
> *Cross your hands at the wrists and put your palms on your chest.*
>
> *Breathe out and uncross your hands as you stretch them out on either side of your body.*

Repeat.

# 33. Catch a ray of sunshine

*A sunny stretch for a rainy day.*

## What you need: space

## What to do:

Ask the children to find a space on their own and to stand with the feet shoulder-width apart.

Use this script to lead the group through the exercise.

> *Bend your knees slightly and sink down a little.*
>
> *Breathe in.*
>
> *Breathe out and lift your left hand over your head. Your palm needs to face upwards towards the sky.*
>
> *While you are doing this, your right hand needs to rest on your thigh with the palm facing towards the ground.*

Repeat, lifting the right arm up and the left arm down.

# 34. Wag your tail like a dog

*This calmer is a pleasurable stretch for everyone.*

## What you need: space

## What to do:

Ask the children to find a space on their own and to stand with the feet shoulder-width apart.

Use this script to lead the group through the exercise.

> *Bend your knees slightly and sink down a little.*
>
> *Breathe in and put your hands on your hips.*
>
> *Breathe out and bend forwards. Keep your back as straight as you can.*
>
> *Turn your head towards the left and your bottom towards the right.*
>
> *Go back to the starting position and repeat on the other side.*

# 35. Push the wall

*This calmer is a controlled, relaxing stretch.*

## What you need: space

## What to do:

Ask the children to find a space on their own and to stand with the feet shoulder- width apart.

Use this script to lead the group through the exercise.

> *Bend your knees slightly and sink down a little.*
>
> *Breathe in.*
>
> *Put your left foot in front of you with the heel on the floor and the toes pointing upward.*
>
> *At the same time, lift both of your hands so that your arms are bent and in front of your chest.*
>
> *Breathe out and push your arms out in front of you.*
>
> *Go back to the beginning position.*

Repeat several times.

# 36. Bouncing frog

*A leg stretch to help everyone feel relaxed and at ease.*

## What you need: space

## What to do:

Ask the children to find a space on their own and to stand with the feet shoulder-width apart.

Use this script to lead the group through the exercise.

> *Bend your knees slightly and sink down a little.*
>
> *Breathe in and put your feet a little wider apart.*
>
> *Breathe out and bend your knees so that you are in a squatting position.*
>
> *Return to the starting position.*

Do this several times.

# 37. Twist your fist

*This calmer is a controlled martial arts movement.*

## What you need: space

## What to do:

Ask the children to find a space on their own and to stand with the feet shoulder-width apart.

Use this script to lead the group through the exercise.

> *Bend your knees slightly and sink down a little.*
>
> *Curl your hands into fists.*
>
> *Bend your elbows.*
>
> *Turn your hands so that your knuckles are facing downwards and your bent fingers are facing upwards.*
>
> *Breathe in.*
>
> *Punch forward with your left fist.*
>
> *Twist it over so that your knuckles are facing upwards and your bent fingers are facing downwards.*
>
> *Go back to the starting position and repeat with the other arm.*

Do this several times.

# 38. Take a walk

*Walking helps to calm both the body and the mind. Take a walk around the playground – or even better, a green, open space.*

## What you need: space

## What to do:

Prompt the children to breathe evenly and slowly and encourage them to swing their arms back and forth. Tell them to try and get a comfortable rhythm going as they walk and ask them not to talk but to concentrate and feel the pleasure of a refreshing walk.

# 39. Lift your fingers

*This calmer is a quick pick-me-up that can be used when your children are over-excited.*

## What you need: space

## What to do:

Use the following script to lead the group in this exercise.

*Sit cross-legged on the floor.*

*Hold your hand up with your fingers in a fist.*

*Breathe in through your nose.*

*Lift up one finger at a time as you silently count one, two, three, four, five.*

*Breathe out slowly through your mouth as you silently count one, two, three, four, five, while folding your fingers, one at a time, back into a fist.*

# 40. Holding a very big ball

*This calmer combines imagination and a controlled, calming stretch.*

## What you need: space; visualization script

## What to do:

Ask the children to find a space on their own and to stand with the feet shoulder-width apart.

Use this script to lead the group through the exercise.

> *Bend your knees slightly and sink down a little.*
> *Breathe in.*
> *Pretend you are holding a very big ball – with one hand on top of the ball and the other hand on the bottom.*
> *Breathe out and change the position of each hand – bottom to top and top to bottom.*

Repeat.

> *Bend your knees slightly and sink down a little.*
> *Put your hands at your sides.*
> *Breathe in.*
> *Move your weight to the left and turn your body to the left.*
> *Put your arms together as if you are saying a prayer and then lift them up and put them on the left side of your face.*
> *Breathe out and go back to the starting position.*

Repeat on the right side.

Do this exercise several times.

# Sensory Calmers

The activities in this section are designed to help children learn ways in which they can use sensory experiences to calm themselves. Together, you will explore ways to manage the classroom environment so that you are able to create a peaceful, composed setting in which purposeful work can take place.

We have all experienced the sense of disorientation, irritation and distraction that occurs when our senses are overloaded. We lose our train of thought and find it impossible to concentrate.

The activities are an antidote for those unsettling feelings. We will show you how to calm different senses in different ways that children will appreciate and can use whenever they feel tense or flustered.

If you do choose to use the calming scents/oil calmers, do make sure that you let the parents know you are going to use them – and can they let you know if any children are allergic!

# 41. Calming touch

*This calmer is an effective quick fix to use whenever you feel your class needs a moment of calm.*

## What you need: nothing

## What to do:

Ask the children to sit very quietly and to shut their eyes.

Tell them to slowly touch their elbows to make sure that they are still there!

Ask them to: gently touch their shoulders to make sure that they are still there and haven't got lost; quietly touch their hair; put their hands in their laps and gently wiggle their toes; gently wiggle their fingers.

Then ask them to breathe quietly for a moment or two, open their eyes and 'come back' to the room.

# 42. A focused moment

*This calmer helps the children to understand that concentrating on our senses is very soothing.*

## What you need: nothing

## What to do:

Sit very still and concentrate your senses on the little details that are usually ignored.

What sounds can you hear?

Which colours can you see?

How do your feet feel in your socks?

Can you feel the softness of your clothes on your shoulders?

You don't need answers, just direct everyone's attention to the small sensations of the moments and they will be instantly calmed.

**Tip:** Go outside and listen to the range of sounds and colours you find in the environment.

# 43. Relaxing aroma

*A calming fragrance can banish anxiety in a moment.*

## What you need: spray bottle or atomizer (from a garden centre or pharmacy), water; suitable essential oil

## What to do:

Choose a suitable scent from the following list:  (you can blend two or more scents if you choose)

- Relaxation     lavender, sandalwood, rose, geranium
- Tension     chamomile, jasmine, rosemary
- Anger     neroli, rosewood, sandalwood
- Anxiety     melissa, clary sage, rosewood

Mix a few drops of the oil with water and fill the atomizer spray and spray the room lightly whenever you feel that your children need to calm down. Give your room a quick spritz every morning and for a calm start to the day.

**Tip:**  Put a small quantity of oil onto a handkerchief for times when you are the one who needs to calm down.  Take a deep inhalation whenever you need a gentle stress-buster or a quick pick-me-up.

# 44. Soft ball soothers

*This calmer is a simple way to soothe frayed nerves.*

## What you need: a collection of colourful soft balls; a bowl

## What to do:

Collect a range of brightly-coloured sponge balls like the ones used for indoor games. Put them in a bowl in the classroom.

Encourage tense children to sit squeezing and unsqueezing a ball as they puzzle over a difficult maths question or feel the need to let off a little nervousness or anger.

# 45. Calming music

*Music draws people together and enables them to share calming experiences.*

## What you need: a selection of instrumental music; CD player

## What to do:

You can utilize the calming effect of music at any time in your setting. Classical music has been found to be the more effective. You can make your own collection and see which composers have the most soothing effect on your children, but here are a few suggestions to get you started:

*Eine Kleine Nachtmusik serenade no 13 by Mozart*

*Suite no 3 (Air on a G string) by Bach*

*Spring Sonata for violin, op 24 ('Spring') by Beethoven*

*Concerto for piano, no 5, op 73 ('Emperor') by Beethoven*

*Sonata for piano no 8, op13 ('Pathetique') by Beethoven*

*Ave Maria or Impromptu no 3, op 142 by Schubert*

**Tip:** Try natural sounds like waves, dolphins, or birdsong that are made specifically to relieve stress, available from our website.

# 46. Treasure box of happiness

*A delightful way to dispel tension.*

## What you need: an attractive box filled with natural 'treasures' – driftwood, feathers, shells, pebbles, happy objects from their past, special photos

## What to do:

When a child is feeling stressed or out-of-sorts, let them sit with the box for a while and examine each thing that is inside.

**Tip:** Allow children to make their own treasure boxes, and whenever they need to cheer up they can spend a minute looking in their box.

# 47. Think steady

*This shows children how calmness gives a sense of being balanced and steady.*

## What you need: space; floor chalk or benches

## What to do:

Talk about how calmness enables us to stay balanced and steady because we are in control of our bodies and minds. Discuss how other emotional states make us feel out of control and unbalanced.

Say that you will show them what you mean.

Draw a line or put a line of benches across the floor.

Ask for a volunteer to be a tightrope walker. Ask them to walk along the line and maybe do some acrobatics as they go along.

When they have done this, you can ask for more volunteers and give them extra tasks:

> walk and sing a gentle song

> walk and shout a loud song

> walk and recite spellings or the alphabet or 9X table.

Discuss whether it was easy or difficult to stay balanced and in control when the extra task was not a calm one.

# Attentive Listening Calmers

Just as our imagined fears and anxieties can make us tense and sick, so our imagination has the power to calm and heal us. When you accompany your children in a guided visualization, you are giving them a route map to places where they can go whenever they feel stressed, tense or anxious.

Visualizations are deeply relaxing because our attention is focused and we are required to sit very still and concentrate on the images that the guide put into our minds. The guide speaks very slowly in a soothing voice and our awareness of the troublesome world fades away as we journey to calm and beautiful places. Then, happily, we can revisit these places whenever we feel the need to reaffirm the wonder of life and whenever we need reassurance and hope.

You can use mood music to enhance the calming effect of the experience and help children to empty their minds of anything except the pleasure of the journey you are sharing.

# 48. Self-esteem booster

*This visualization raises morale and calms anxiety.*

## What you need: rain stick or mood music on CD

## What to do:

Give the children some time to think about how special they are. Ask them to close their eyes and put their hands on their knees with the palms facing upwards and their fingers lightly curled.

Using a rain stick or mood music, give them time to think about what makes them special. Most children find it easy to sit in this position because it relaxes their shoulders.

Tip: Step-by-step, build on this activity and teach your class how to create personalised creative visualizations so that they can find peace, calm and motivation independently.

# 49. Before a test

*This visualization helps children calm themselves before a test.*

## What you need: visualization script

## What to do:

Read the following script in a calm voice, pausing often.

*Say it to yourself and all your fears fly away. You feel proud of yourself because you know that you are working hard and doing your best.*

*Sit with both feet on the floor. Make sure you are comfortable and warm and will not be disturbed.*
*Close your eyes and sit very still.*
*Listen to your breathing. Can you feel the air going in and out? Just listen to your breath for a moment and let your mind become very still.*

*You are in a room full of people but it is very quiet. You are sitting in the classroom and there is a piece of paper in front of you. Your pencil case is on the table and all the pencils and pens are ready for you to use them. You feel calm and ready and you know that you are going to do your best.*

*You work steadily, one question at a time. Your mind is clear and you feel calm and your memory is working well. Tell yourself you can do this.*

*Now it is time for you to bring your mind back to the classroom. Take a long deep breath and begin to notice sounds around you.*
*Open your eyes when you are ready and sit quietly for a moment.*
*Remember the calm feeling and keep it in your head as we do the test today.*

# 50. The garden

*This visualization could be used to calm children after they have had a stressful experience.*

## What you need: visualization script

## What to do:

Read the following script in a calm voice, pausing often:

> *Sit with both feet on the floor. Make sure you are comfortable and warm and will not be disturbed.*
>
> *Take a long slow breath and let it out very gently, like this. Your breathing is slow and calm. Your mind is calm. Calm and slow. Calm and relaxed.*
>
> *You are walking in a beautiful garden. Can you see all the flowers? What colours are they? Can you smell them?*
>
> *Look up into the sky. Can you see little white clouds or is the sky very blue? You feel very calm and happy.*
>
> *It is a very big garden. How far away can you see? Can you see trees in the distance? The sun is shining. You are quite safe here.*
>
> *Now it is time to come back to the classroom. Take your time. Breathe deeply. Begin to notice the sounds around you.*
>
> *Wiggle your fingers and toes. When you are ready, you can open your eyes.*

# 51. Preparing for social situations

*This creative visualisation is designed to help children feel confident about going to a new school.*

## What you need: visualization script

## What to do:

Read the following script in a calm voice, pausing often.

*Close your eyes and sit very still.*

*You see the door to your new school and walk towards it. Your heartbeat is steady and calm. You walk through the door. Your breathing is steady and calm.*

*You walk up the corridor. Your forehead is cool and clear. You feel happy and confident. In your head, you repeat to yourself, "I am confident. I am relaxed. I am confident. I am relaxed." You say this to yourself as you walk up the corridor.*

*You know that everyone is looking at you but you feel calm and relaxed. You smile at them and notice that they look friendly. You feel confident and happy.*

*Now it is time to come back to this classroom. Take your time. Breathe deeply. Begin to notice the sounds around you.*

*Wiggle your fingers and toes. When you are ready, you can open your eyes*

# 52. Blow your worries away

*This visualization teaches children an excellent technique for minimizing their anxieties.*

## What you need: visualization script

## What to do:

Read the following script in a calm voice, pausing often.

*Sit still with your hands resting gently in your lap. Close your eyes and concentrate on your breathing. Feel it moving slowly in and out, in and out.*

*Imagine you have a balloon in your hands. Feel it stretchy and rubbery in your hands. What colour is your balloon? What shape is it?*

*In your imagination, I want you to pick up the balloon and get ready to blow it up. Take a deep breath. As you breathe in, feel that you are breathing in happiness. Hold your breath for a moment.*

*As you blow your breath out, imagine that you are blowing all of your worries into the balloon.*

*Now breathe in some more happiness and blow any thoughts that are making you unhappy. Blow your unhappy thoughts into the balloon.*

*Hold up the big balloon full of worries and unhappiness. Hold it high above your head. Feel the wind take the balloon and let it go.*

*Now get ready to come back to the classroom. Roll your shoulders round and round and relax your neck. When you are ready, you can open your eyes and smile at the person next to you.*

# 53. The shower of light

*This calming visualization is designed to help children feel a strong sense of well-being and good health.*

## What you need: visualization script

## What to do:

Read the following script in a calm voice, pausing often.

> *Sit still with your hands resting gently in your lap. Close your eyes and concentrate on your breathing. Feel it moving slowly in and out, in and out.*
> *You feel something warm and wonderful on your head and shoulders. It makes you feel calm and full of joy.*
>
> *You look up to see where it is coming from and realize that you are standing in a shower of magic blue light. It is pouring down from the sky: a shower of blue light that sparkles and glitters.*
>
> *It is a shower of special light. It is pouring health and happiness all over you. You feel strong and well and happy. Your skin feels soft and warm.*
> *Feel the sparkling blue light pouring inside of you – through your mouth and skin. Inside you feel well and strong and full of light. You are filling up with warm, blue light.*
>
> *Enjoy the feeling for a little while longer and then slowly make your way back to the classroom.*
>
> *When you are ready, you can open your eyes and give your legs a shake and a stretch.*

# 54. Relaxing place

*Remembering a relaxing place reduces anxiety about forthcoming events or situations.*

## What you need: nothing

## What to do:

Read the following script in a calm voice, pausing often.

*Sit still with your hands resting gently in your lap. Close your eyes and concentrate on your breathing. Feel it moving slowly in and out, in and out.*

*Now I want you to remember a place where you felt happy and calm and relaxed. It might be at home, or in the garden or maybe a day on your holidays when you were on the beach. Take a minute to choose your favourite memory.*

*When you find it I want you to say to yourself (silently), "I feel very warm. I feel very relaxed. I feel very calm."*

*Now try to make your memory as real as possible. I want you to remember with all of your senses. What can you see?*

*Now that you are feeling relaxed and calm, I want you to begin to come back to the classroom. Bring back with you that feeling of being relaxed and calm as you take a deep breath, and slowly bring yourself back to 'the here and now'. Open your eyes when you are ready and sit quiet and still for a moment.*

# 55. Goal-setting visualization

*Positive visualization of future success is one of the keys to achieving our goals.*

## What you need: nothing

## What to do:

Read the following script in a calm voice, pausing often.

*Sit still with your hands resting gently in your lap. Close your eyes and concentrate on your breathing. Feel it moving slowly in and out, in and out. Think about something you want to be good at.*

*Now I want you to use your imagination to make a picture inside your head. Imagine yourself being very successful at the thing you have chosen. Imagine yourself doing it really well. Say to yourself, "I am doing really well. I am strong and clever and successful."*

*Enjoy the good feeling of success for a while and then begin to bring yourself back to the classroom. Remember to bring that good feeling back with you! Shake your arms and legs and take a deep breath. Open your eyes when you are ready and smile at the rest of the class. Hold on to the good feeling that your imagination has given you.*

# 56. Flying

*This visualization relieves tension by taking the class on a magical journey to wherever they wish to go.*

## What you need: nothing

## What to do:

Read the following script in a calm voice, pausing often.

*Sit still with your hands resting gently in your lap. Close your eyes and concentrate on your breathing. Feel it moving slowly in and out, in and out. Breathe deeply from your stomach, not just from your chest. Inhale slowly through your nose while I count to 3.*

*Now exhale slowly through your mouth while I count to 3.*

*I want you to imagine that you are a bird.*
*You are flying up into the sky. The sun is shining on your feathers and you feel light and happy. Feel the soft breeze on your feathers. You can fly as far and as high as you wish. You are free.*

*As you fly, you look down and see some wonderful sights. What do you see?*

*Now you are flying home. What can you see?*

*Now you need to fly back to the classroom. You are pleased to be back with all the familiar friends in your class team. See how many eyes you can smile into by the time I quietly count to 5.*

*Now I would like you all to smile into my eyes and then we can go on to our next activity.*

# 57. Big bottle of calm

*This activity allows children to use their imagination as they let go of pent-up anxiety or stress, let off steam and calm down gently.*

## What you need: nothing

## What to do:

Ask everyone to stand up.

Tell them that they are each holding a huge bottle.

Ask them to hold the heavy bottle and to reach up to the big screw top.

The top is stuck and they need to struggle to remove it. Encourage them to act out the strenuous stretching activity. Give instructions like: Push harder, try to turn the big stopper.

Talk them through turning the cap very slowly by saying things like, *Slowly, slowly, the top is getting looser. Good, keep going.*

Then ask the children to put the imaginary top on their table.

Now wafts of wonderful calming scent float out of the bottle and drift down all over each child, making them feel warm, relaxed and happy.

Let them feel the calming effect as the perfume gently covers them. What does it smell like? Lavender? Candy floss? Strawberries? Allow each child to choose their own soothing perfume.

Feel the warmth of calm as it goes inside and soothes their whole body.
Take five, slow, deep breaths and then, gently, ask them to sit down and resume their lesson.

# 58. The snowmen are here

*This calmer helps children learn essential relaxation techniques in an enjoyable way.*

## What you need: nothing

## What to do:

Ask the children to stand up.

Tell them that it is very cold. Ask them to act out the feeling of being freezing cold. Now introduce the idea of building a snowman. Describe how this is done with a big ball of snow.

Ask them to build themselves into snowmen by pretending to scoop up heavy lumps of cold snow and press it on to different parts of their bodies.

Now ask them to stand very tall and still just like a snowman.

Tell the class that the weather is getting warmer. The snowman must slowly melt. Ask the children to relax and feel their snow bodies become floppier and softer as they sink gently into their seats and rest their heads on the table.

Allow them to sit for a few minutes in this relaxed state before resuming your normal classroom activities.

# 59. The tree

*This visualization is about how it must feel to be a tree in the sunshine.*

## What you need: visualization script

## What to do:

Guide the group through the visualization, pausing often.

*Sit with both feet on the floor. Make sure you are comfortable and warm and will not be disturbed. Close your eyes and sit very still.*

*Listen to your breathing. Can you feel the air going in and out? Just listen to your breath for a moment and let your mind become very still.*

*Take a long, slow breath and let it out very gently, like this. Your breathing is slow and calm. Your mind is calm. Calm and slow. Calm and relaxed. Think about your feet. Make sure that they are very flat on the floor.*

*Pretend that you are a tree and the roots of the tree are growing down into the ground. They are strong and they are going deep, deep into the earth that feeds them with water from the raindrops.*

*You are a beautiful tree and you can feel the gentle breeze blowing all around your branches. You are a strong tree and all of your leaves are green and bright.*

*A little bird comes to sit in your branches and it sings a lovely little song. The bird is very happy to be in your tree. It sings because it is happy. The bird has feathers of many bright colours.*

*Now it is time for you to turn back into a boy or girl again. Gently let the bird fly away to another tree. Watch it fly away in the sunlight.*

*Shake your shoulders and arms.*
*Wiggle your fingers and toes.*
*Wiggle your knees and elbows.*
*Open your eyes when you are ready and sit quietly for a moment.*

# 60. Just imagine

*This visualization encourages positive thinking.*

## What you need: nothing

## What to do:

Make a list of relaxed things – ice cream melting in the sun, a dog asleep in the shade, a lizard on a rock in the desert, a fluffy pink cushion.

Ask the group to imagine that they are one of these things for a few minutes every time you need them to relax and calm down.

You can keep a list of floppy, relaxed things and ask the group to add to the list whenever they think of a new thing to imagine.

# 61. Affirmative calm

*This affirmation helps children to feel calm and positive.*

## What you need: nothing

## What to do:

Explain that repeating affirmations helps each of us to stay positive and calm.
They are always stated in the present tense and they are always positive.
Ask the group to try these affirmations.

- I can work well today.

- I feel calm.

- I feel peaceful today.

- I share calm with everyone I meet.

Put the children into small groups and ask them to think of more affirmations to share with one another.

Make them into posters to put on the wall or take home.

# 62. Indoor country walk

*This is a great, wet day calmer.*

## What you need: space

## What to do:

Ask the group to accompany you on an indoor country walk by lining up behind you.

Ask them to copy you as you talk them through the walk. Like this:

> *Walk lightly on springy grass.*
> *Step carefully across a stream.*
> *Open and close gates.*
> *Look at cows and flowers.*
> *Go into a wood and move among the trees.*
> *Take a dog with you and throw sticks,*

etc.
Let a volunteer lead the group on a sunny beach walk.

# 63. Ice age

*This musical calmer never fails to cool everyone down.*

## What you need: space; peaceful music

## What to do:

Ask everyone to stand in a circle.

Tell them that the Ice Age has returned and they are frozen solid and cannot move. Play the peaceful music.

Name one part of the body and announce that this is thawing out and can move – e.g. fingers. Tell them that they can move that part of their body in any way they like. One at a time, thaw out more body parts – e.g. hands, toes, elbows, knees and so on.

Slowly, their whole bodies will have thawed out and they will be ready for the next activity.

**Tip:** Choose one child to be leader and choose the movements, while the others imitate what he/she does.

# 64. Feel the weight

*Slow movements are very calming.*

## What you need: space

## What to do:

Ask everyone to find a space. Tell them to stand still with their feet apart.

Now ask them to imagine that they are weight-lifters and to slowly lift a very heavy weight. This movement needs to be controlled and careful.

Then they must carefully lower the weight so that it touches the ground without hurting anyone.

Then ask the group to feel the lightness of their bodies. They can float around the space for a while until you call, *Lift the weight,* when they must stop and do another weight lift. Continue until they are calm and relaxed.

**Tip:** The activity can be made more challenging if you put the group into pairs and ask them to work on a presentation of a set of balancing scales. One partner stretches tall as they become lighter while the other becomes heavier and sinks to the ground.

# Interactive Calmers

Warmth is a very supportive and reassuring feeling and we all know the joy of curling up somewhere warm and safe when the world seems grey and hostile.

In these light-hearted activities, children interact with familiar things or friends to share the warmth of calm through smiles and simple co-operative games.

Each activity is designed to promote friendliness and a refreshing sense of being part of a group that does simple, joyful things as a team. They are non-competitive so everyone can lower their guard, relax and just take pleasure in the moment.

There is a wide range of activities in this section, so you are sure to find some that suit the nature of your particular group or setting.

# 65. Pass a smile

*This calmer is a joyful, calming ritual for any time of the day.*

## What you need: nothing

## What to do:

Smile at one of your children, who should then pass the smile on to another child until it has been given to every child in the class.

If you add more welcoming activities like shaking hands, saying, *Hello, how are you? Have a good day*, and so on, you will have developed a wonderfully calming ritual with which to begin your lessons.

# 66. Calming support

*A reassuring sense of calm develops when we know that we are supported.*

## What you need: nothing

## What to do:

Say that you are looking for ways to make the classroom calmer and happier and you would appreciate everyone's help.

Use a sentence starter like the ones that follow:

*At school, I feel left out when …………..*
*I feel worried when ……..*
*I feel lonely when ……………….*

Then ask children to respond by using another sentence starter:

*Would it help if ……?*

**Tip:** Incorporate this system of question and answer into your circle time sessions and PSHE lessons.

# 67. The happy hat

*This calmer creates a feel-good atmosphere and is useful if children are disheartened*

## What you need: a brightly coloured hat (it could be a striped bobble hat or a summery straw hat)

## What to do:

When you feel that the class needs brightening up or de-stressing, say, *I think we need that happy hat.*

Walk around the room holding the happy hat.

Choose a child and put the hat on their head.

Ask the wearer of the happy hat to think of something that they would like the group to think about for a moment.

The child can say anything they like but it must be a happy thought. For instance, they might say, *I am thinking of our class trip when we all went on the coach to the seaside and had our sandwiches on the beach* or, *I am thinking about clowns and how they make me laugh,* or *I am thinking of a good joke I heard yesterday, would you like to hear it?*

Encourage the children to be inventive and amusing.

# 68. Heads down, thumbs up

*This is a useful calmer if you find that you have a few restless moments at the end of a lesson.*

## What you need: nothing

## What to do:

Choose three or four players to wait at the front of the room.

Call out, *Heads down, thumbs up.* The seated children then put their heads down, close their eyes and put their fists on their ears with their thumbs sticking out.

The standing children then walk very quietly round the room and choose one person each by gently gripping their thumbs.

When a classmate is touched in this way, they must fold their thumbs into their fists to indicate that they have been chosen. (It is important that children who are observed to be peeping or keeping their eyes open are NOT chosen.)

The 'walkers' return to the front of the room when they have selected a child.
You then need to call out, *Heads up,* and all the players can open their eyes and look up.

The players who were touched must then try to guess which of the 'walkers' has chosen them. To give everyone an equal chance, it is important that the walkers do not indicate if a guess is right or not until everyone has had their turn at guessing. The children who have guessed correctly swap places with their 'walker' and the game continues.

# 69. Five spots

*The game is an engaging way to fill those times when children are waiting for the bell and can become restless.*

## What you need: blackboard, whiteboard or flip chart

## What to do:

Everyone sits in their place looking at the whiteboard.

One child is chosen to come forward and put five dots anywhere on the whiteboard.

A second child is chosen to come forward and draw a person with head, hands and feet touching a different dot. Encourage them to be inventive.

If there is time, you can ask for positive comments about neatness, cleverness, humour, etc.

# 70. Down the line

*This calmer is a quiet game for a spare moment.*

## What you need: nothing

## What to do:

Whisper a phrase to the person sitting to your right. For instance, *She sells seashells on the seashore.* Say it once only.

This person then whispers it to the person sitting to his/her right.

This continues until everyone has had a turn.

The last person then repeats the sentence aloud and you repeat the original sentence.

# 71. Write yourself calm

*This calmer is effective because writing things down helps each of us to order our thoughts and feelings.*

## What you need: a small notebook for each child; a safe place to keep these books

## What to do:

Give each child a notebook/journal.

Explain clearly that this will be a very private notebook and that each journal will be kept in a safe place.

When you notice that a child is distressed or off-balance, give them the opportunity to sit somewhere quiet and write in their private journal.

Alternatively, if children distrust the idea of committing their feelings to a journal, give unsettled children a piece of paper and allow them to write about their feelings and tell them that they can tear up what they have written so that they have the security of knowing that they have expressed themselves in absolute safety.

# 72. Focusing on solutions

*This calmer focuses on positive thinking.*

## What you need: paper and pencils; flip chart

## What to do:

Ask the group to sit quietly.

Tell them that this is a private activity that they can choose not to share.
Give everyone a piece of paper and a pencil.

Write, *I want to* ……………… on the flip-chart and ask the group to complete the sentence by thinking of one problem they would like to solve in the near future and writing it down on their piece of paper. This can be anything that is important to them; for example, *I want to have more friends or I want to learn my tables.*

Then ask them to write a list of small things that they are able to do to make the thing they want happen.

Ask them to order the list so that it becomes a series of small steps that take them in the right direction.

Tell them to choose one step from their list and to decide that they will take that one small step immediately.

Later, you can encourage them to review their progress by reflecting on how that first small step has made them feel and what they learned from taking it. Then you can ask them to choose a second step from their list.

**Tip:** Use the same process to solve group problems through discussion and debate. This helps each member of the group to see how the process works and to learn more about problem solving from each other.

# 73. Growing calm feelings

*Making a garden of calm is a very enriching and absorbing activity.*

## What you need: paper; crayons or paints

## What to do:

Give out the paper and ask the group to draw some beautiful flowers.

Tell them to write calm words all around the flower.  Ask them to use different colours.

Make a garden of calm flowers and calming words and use for a wall display.

# 74. Can do, can't do

*A game that teaches patience and the necessity of staying calm and waiting your turn.*

## What you need: nothing

## What to do:

Show the group some things that you can do at the same time; for example, scratch your head and close your eyes.

Show them some things that you can't do at the same time; for example, bend your knees and stretch up to the ceiling.

Ask them to think of examples of each to show the rest of the group.
Take turns so that everyone can show examples of can dos and can't dos.

Use these to point out there are many things that teachers can't do at the same time – e.g. help Sara with her spelling and find the lost rulers. Explain that this is why they need to stay quiet and calm and be patient sometimes.

# 75. Support the supporters

*When each member feels supported and secure, the group works together calmly.*

## What you need: nothing

## What to do:

Take note of the times when classmates help and support one another.

These examples of group support need to be praised and rewarded so make a point of mentioning them whenever they arise by saying things like, *During the history lesson, I noticed that Kelly helped Suzanne to find the book she needed. That was a good thing to do and I think Kelly showed how mature and helpful she is. Let's give her a clap.*

Make badges and certificates to praise supportive behaviour.

Ask the group to nominate each other and cite examples of calming, group-building behaviour.

# 76. Don't fret about the future

*Calmness comes from worrying less about what might happen and focusing on enjoying the present.*

## What you need: nothing

## What to do:

Ask the group to share some of the things they worry about.

Group these into 'now worries we can help with' and 'worries about things that might happen in the future'.

Share solutions for 'now' worries and discuss the fact that there is no point in worrying what might happen because it might not!

Decide, as a group, to focus on what is happening now, and to let the future take care of itself – everyone will feel much calmer.

# 77. Half empty or half full?

*Reframing is a strategy for changing the way we look at life. It helps us to see things in a positive, calm way.*

## What you need: nothing

## What to do:

Explain that reframing is a way to understand that there are many ways to interpret the same situation.

It helps us to get rid of negative thoughts and replace them with positive ones. You do four things:

1.   make an effort to see things positively
2.   eliminate negative thoughts
3.   use affirmations
4.   enjoy each moment.

Give the group some situations:

*   You get into the canteen and there are no dinners left that you like.
*   Your best friend is moving a long way away.
*   It is raining so football will be cancelled.

Help the group to make lists of the variety of ways in which we could reframe these events.

# 78. The art of peace

*This calmer focuses on attentive looking.*

**What you need:** pictures of Picasso doves (available on the internet) or you could use any other painting which conveys a feeling of calm

## What to do:

Allow the children time to study the pictures and then ask them to talk about what it is in the picture that makes you think of calmness. It may be by association of some object in the picture, the colours used, the soft shapes, or the activity portrayed.

**Tip:** Children can write down their ideas, decorate them and make their observations into a wall display.

# 79. Calm haiku

*This is a special way to write about calm.*

## What you need: flip chart; paper; pencils

## What to do:

Describe the structure of a haiku – put simply, it is a short poem of three lines.

The first and third lines have 5 syllables and the middle line has 7 syllables.

Show the group this example of a haiku about calm:

> Tonight a gentle
> Calm is floating all around.
> The moon is smiling.

Make a collection of words and phrases that describe calm.

Ask the children to write their own haiku about calm.

# 80. How calm feels inside

*This helps children to share the sensations of calm.*

## What you need: outline of a human figure (one for each child); pencils; crayons; flip chart

## What to do:

Make a list of different emotions and ask volunteers to describe the physical sensations we experience when we feel each one. Save the sensations of calm until the end of the discussion.

Give each child a copy of the outline of a human figure.

Ask them to draw in the sensations – hands feeling just a little bit floppy, breathing slow, toes relaxed, etc.

Ask them to surround the figure with things that make them feel calm and relaxed – sunshine, floppy cushion, cup of cocoa, etc.

# 81. Pass it on

*This is a fun way to share calming strategies and see which are appropriate to different situations.*

## What you need: paper; pencils; flip chart

## What to do:

Ask the group to help you make a list of calming strategies on the flip chart.

Give every child a piece of paper and ask them to write the name of a creature at the top of the paper.

They then need to fold the paper over so that no-one can see what they have written. The paper is passed to another child who writes a problem on the paper, which is again folded and passed on.

The third child writes down a calming strategy.

The paper is passed on and the fourth child reads out the whole piece of paper. They may read like this:

1.    A bumble bee
2.    had to do a spelling test
3.    so he did some yoga.

With each reading, you can discuss if the calming strategy was a good one to choose.

**Tip:** The pieces of paper can be developed to become a collection of stories.

# 82. Calm verbs

*Word-building helps children understand that calm is something that we 'do'.*

## What you need: paper; pencils; flip chart

## What to do:

Look up 'calm' in a thesaurus. Talk about these words so that their meaning is clear.

Pacify
Placate
Appease
Soothe
Relax
Lull
Tranquillize
Hush

Let them choose an animal and then write a humorous set of instructions like this:

How to pacify an angry giraffe.
How to soothe an agitated lion.
How to hush a flock of excited parrots.
How to calm a worried wombat.

Make cartoon pictures to go with the 'how to' writing.

# 83. Calm objects

*This activity helps children to 'see' calm in a symbolic way.*

## What you need: fabric; cereal packets; paints; paper; papier-mâché or clay; pictures of calm sculptures and artworks

## What to do:

Tell the group that you want them to make an object that will make people feel calm when they see or touch it.

Show them examples of sculpture and ask them to decide if they are calming or exciting. Discuss the qualities of calm and decide on some general rules that would apply to the object they will make. These could include:

> Colour – pale blue, cream, pale yellow, white.
> Texture – smooth or soft.
> Shape – simple, rounded.
> No spiky bits or wild colours or hard edges.

Ask them to work in groups to create a calming object.
Discuss which finished objects meet the criteria you have agreed upon.
Make a display of your calming objects.

**Tip:** Use the internet to investigate sculptors who make calming works of art and ask groups to make presentations to show their work.

# 84. Worry beads

*Worry beads are used all over the world to help people calm down.*

## What you need: big beads; string

## What to do:

Make some strings of worry beads. These are strings of fairly big beads that are strung loosely on a piece of string that is long enough for the beads to be moved up and down the string. Your group may like to make some themselves and then they can 'play' with them whenever they feel tense or upset.

**Tip:** You could make one big one – where each child in the class puts a bead on to make a necklace. Whenever you want to visualize the class supporting you, you put on the necklace.

# 85. Flag it up

*Children need to know how to find support from other people when they feel angry, worried or sad.*

## What you need: paper and straws

## What to do:

Make simple, triangular flags from straws and paper. Let the group colour them in.

Make a list of relevant questions, like: *If you are feeling upset, what can you do?*

Then say, *Flag up.*

Children who know the answer then hold up their flag and offer a solution.

Work through your list and then ask children to share worries of their own.

Ask children to offer support by suggesting helpful strategies and techniques.

# 86. Recipe for calm

*Putting all the ingredients together to make a calm life.*

## What you need: specimen recipes

## What to do:

Look at the recipes and note how they are constructed: ingredients, method, etc.

Make a list of possible ingredients of calmness.

Discuss ways in which these ingredients might be combined.

Write the recipe for calm.

# 87. Chunking

*Teach your children to break tasks down into smaller parts and you will be teaching them how to stay calm and confident.*

## What you need: flip chart

## What to do:

Draw a number-line on your white/blackboard.

Choose an area of the curriculum.

Choose a specific task and show the children how it can be split into a series of chunks that build up to a completed task.

Follow the same procedure with other lessons or courses of study so that the group can see that learning is not overwhelmingly huge but a series of smaller tasks that build up towards success and competency.

# 88. Mrs Brown's rabbit

*Cuddly toys are a good way to calm very young children.*

## What you need: cuddly toy for each child plus one rabbit (real or toy)

## What to do:

Give every child a cuddly toy.

Show them the cuddly rabbit and say, *This is Mrs Brown's rabbit, Boxer. He likes to have his ears stroked.*

Stroke the rabbit's ears and ask everyone to copy you with their cuddly toy.

Now go round the group and ask each child to introduce their cuddly toy and demonstrate what it likes.

# 89. Colours and emotions

*This calmer will help your children to make associations between colour and emotion.*

## What you need: paper; paints, or coloured crayons

## What to do:

Discuss emotions with the group. Make a list of the different emotions and list how these emotions make us feel inside and how they show up in our behaviour.

Ask the group to choose either the emotion of anger or the feeling of calm and draw or paint what this emotion feels like.

Tell them to try to feel the emotion as they paint or draw – a picture about anger will look spiky and hot whereas a picture of calm will look more floaty and fluid, perhaps. Ask them to think carefully about the colours they choose.

When the pictures are finished, group them so that the same emotions are put together. Ask everyone to compare these pictures and to look for similarities in the way that the emotion has been portrayed.

# 90. Drawing to music

*This activity helps children to relax because it combines listening to music with a gentle physical activity.*

## What you need: jotters and pencils, or paper and paints/crayons; calming music

## What to do:

Give the group the equipment they need or ask them to find their jotter and a pencil. Explain that you are going to play some music.

Ask them to listen to the music and, when they are ready, to draw patterns to show how the music sounds and how it makes them feel.

If you have given them colours, you need to explain that they must choose or mix colours very carefully so that the colours correspond with the sounds that the music is making.

Tell them that you do not want pictures of actual things – it is a mood that you want to see and they need to just let the pencil or brush move by itself to the flow and rhythm of the music.

Now play the music and allow it to guide everyone's hands towards the creation of peaceful, calming patterns.

# 91. Positively calm

*When we think and feel in a constructive and positive way, we are automatically much calmer than when we think negative thoughts.*

## What you need: box or bag containing cards upon which are written the names of every child in your class or group

## What to do:

Keep the box on your desk and use it when you feel that the class needs a boost.

Take one card out of the box and call out the child's name. This is the child who will receive affirmative feedback from his/her classmates.

Take out another card and ask the named child to say something really positive about the first child. This could be a good point about their personality, a comment on something they are good at or could refer to an interesting out-of-school activity.

Take out another name and ask the named child to also say something positive. Repeat this with a third child.

**Tip:** It is a good idea to mark the first child's card with the date so that you can ensure that every child gets a turn at receiving positive feedback.

# 92. Getting to know an atlas

*Atlases give children hours of meaningful calm activity.*

## What you need: a range of atlases

## What to do:

Many children are able to concentrate on an atlas for long periods of time and find the activity engrossing and calming.

Give out the atlases and allow free investigation.

Then this can become more task-oriented as you give directions for study like: *Can you find the longest river in South America?* or, *Who can name two countries that lie alongside France?* etc.

**Tip:** Ask the group to invent an 'atlas quiz-book' for other classes to use.

# 93. Calm water

*This calmer also works as a vocabulary extension activity.*

## What you need: paper; paints/crayons; pencils; flip chart pictures of calm and stormy water

## What to do:

Show the group a picture of calm water.
Make a list of words to describe the scene:
> Smooth
> Flat
> Still
> Motionless
> Undisturbed.

Show them a picture of stormy water.
Make a list of appropriate words.
> Stormy
> Tempestuous
> Wild
> Raging
> Furious
> Turbulent
> Squally
> Windy
> Gusty
> Choppy
> Blustery.

Ask them to choose one set of words and create a picture of their own, or, ask them to write a poem to describe their picture in words and make a display of pictures and words.

# 94. Calm sounds

*This activity investigates the quiet sounds of calm.*

## What you need: paper; pencils; musical instruments; flip chart

## What to do:

Ask groups to work together to find 8 different calming sounds. They can use musical instruments or their own voices.

When they have found the sounds, their task is to devise ways of writing them down so that their sound and a sense of their calmness is conveyed. Some, like *shhhhh* will be familiar but others will require more thought.

Ask the children to play each of the sounds to the whole class, and describe what they did. Then ask for volunteers from the listeners to come forward and recreate the sounds.

# 95. Button box

*This calmer allows children to spend time sorting buttons, a pastime that they find very soothing.*

## What you need: a variety of old buttons in a box

## What to do:

This is a very simple activity. All you need to do is give the child the box of buttons and the child decides to sort the buttons in any way they like.

**Tip:** Make collections of other objects and keep them ready for occasions when particular children need a time of calm.

# 96. Picture postcards

*This calmer helps you make every day feel like a holiday.*

## What you need: a collection of holiday postcards, posters or pictures from magazines and holiday brochures; paints; paper

## What to do:

Share the pictures with your group.

Ask the group to look at them and prompt them to notice the calmness and peacefulness of the views. Talk about how the landscapes they portray are quiet and free from hustle and bustle.

Use this information as a stimulus for paintings that are equally calm and peaceful.

Ask each child to choose their favourite picture postcard and to study it intently so that they can keep the image inside their head and think of it whenever they feel the need to find a peaceful place to calm down in.

# 97. Colour hunting

*Focusing the group's attention is an excellent way to create calm and thoughtfulness.*

## What you need: colour charts from any DIY store

## What to do:

Put the children into pairs or small groups.

Cut up the colour chart and stick on card so that each child has a range of five or six colours.

Choose a location – this can be inside in the classroom or library, etc. or outside in the open air.

Hand out the charts and ask each group to find something that is as close as possible to the colours they have been given.

Allow time to discuss the task so that children can describe the experience of colour hunting.

# 98. Balmy weather

*This activity extends children's awareness of expressive language.*

## What you need: paper; pencils; crayons; flip chart

## What to do:

Talk about the weather and collect words that are used to describe it. Make these words into two lists – CALM weather and STORMY weather.

Talk about these lists and ask children to repeat the words in ways that show their meaning – loud, sharp voice for stormy words and slow, flat voice for calm words.

Talk about how we can use words to paint pictures in our minds. Use this poem from Ancient Egypt as an example of how this is done:

> **Poem to the Sun**
> All the cattle are resting in the fields,
> The trees and the plants are growing,
> The birds flutter above the marshes,
> Their wings are uplifted in adoration.
> And all the sheep are dancing,
> All the winged things are flying,
> They live when you have shone on them.
>
> The boats sail upstream and downstream alike,
> Every highway is open because you dawn.
> The fish in the river leap up in front of you,
> Your rays are in the middle of the great green sea.

Allow the children to draw or paint an illustration of the calm scene that this poem describes, or write their own group poem to describe calm, balmy weather.

# 99. Pass the squeeze

*This calmer is a friendly way to encourage gentle, physical contact.*

## What you need: nothing

## What to do:

Sit the class in the quiet corner and ask everyone to join hands and close their eyes.

Gently squeeze the hand of the child on your left, who then gently squeezes the hand of the child on his left and so on until the 'squeeze' has passed around the group and back to you.

**Tip:** Pass a fluffy ball or toy around the room in the same way.

# 100. Boundary walk

*This activity takes time but works because a gentle walk is always calming.*

## What you need: magnifying glasses; notepads/clip boards; pencils (optional)

## What to do:

Tell the group that they are going on a short journey.

Explain that you want them to find as many interesting things as possible by looking very closely and concentrating on what they are doing.

Take them on a slow walk around the boundary of your setting and ask them to find as many interesting things as possible by looking high and low.

Ask them to keep a list of the things that they notice. This may be bits of litter, insects, plants, colours, textures. You will be amazed at the extent of the group's observations as they move slowly around your school boundary. If your setting is bounded by a hedge, you can ask the group to make a detailed study of the range of plants that live under the hedge.

# 101. Magical squares

*This calmer is an absorbing activity to calm your group on a hot day.*

## What you need: a grassy area; metre stick; string or wool; lolly sticks (four per group); clip boards; paper; pencils; plastic containers (optional)

## What to do:

Put the children into small groups.

Mark out a square metre for each group using lolly sticks to mark the corners and string to make the boundary line.

Give the groups a time restraint, e.g. 20 minutes, and ask them to list the variety of things they can find in the square during that time – different plants, tiny stones, litter, etc.

If you wish, you can allow them to make a collection of items (but not live creatures!). Alternatively, they can draw each different plant.

Give them time to present their findings and express their amazement at just how much they are able to find.

# 102. Into the unknown.

*This game helps children stay calm whilst being adventurous.*

**What you need:** a blanket or large cloth; a number of different objects from around the room

## What to do:

Spread the objects across the floor and cover them with the blanket.

Choose a child to wriggle under the blanket and bring out an object.

Ask them to show the group what they have found and ask them to talk a little about how it felt to be under the blanket.

Repeat with other children until all the objects have been retrieved.

**Tip:** Ask the children to invent a character who is afraid of the dark and to write a story about the character's adventures.

# Artistic Calmers

Calm is a feeling of quiet happiness and self-control and these activities will help you restore them to that kind of feeling when tempers have become frayed, and everyone needs to settle down and cheer up.

This section is full of ideas to help children wind down with words, music and drama. The activities are useful for wet days when everyone is cooped up indoors and children become restless and need to let off steam in a controlled and positive manner.

Try them out whenever you want to change the atmosphere in your setting and see how they can fill even the greyest day with warmth and sunshine.

In the drama calmers, children act out situations and solutions that help them to learn how to manage negative feelings and, most importantly, how each of us has the power to control our emotions and find our way back to serenity when we are in danger of losing our tempers or our equilibrium.

Some activities show children just how useful our imagination can be whilst others develop empathy so that they don't feel that they are the only ones who struggle to control difficult feelings.

Few props are needed to enjoy these activities and they are such fun that your children will want to play them over and over again.

# 103. First and last names

*An inclusive calmer for people who don't know each other well.*

## What you need: nothing

## What to do:

Using the initial of their first and surnames, the children have to respond to the questions that you ask. For example, *John Brown, what is your special food?* John could answer, *Juicy beans, Jumpy beetroot* or *Jelly bears* and so on. (Make sure you have a selection of questions ready: holiday destination, hobby, game, etc.)

As they say their name, each child claps the syllable rhythm of their name.

# 104. Humming walk

*Humming together is a very calming activity.*

## What you need: nothing

## What to do:

Teach the group a little humming tune and ask them to join in.

Make funny faces as you hum and indicate that you want them to copy you.

Walk around the room and continue humming. If you touch a child on the back they must follow you and continue humming.

Lie down on the floor and let them join you as you hum at the ceiling.

Get up and continue your walk, using hand signals beckoning the group to join you.

Take them back to their seats and continue to hum until everyone is seated and calm.

# 105. Follow me

*A simple song/chant that will focus and calm children as they follow you,
line by line.*

## What you need: nothing

## What to do:

Ask the group to repeat each line as you chant it.

**Bill Grogan's goat**
*There was a man
(There was a man)
Now please take note
(Now please take note)
There was a man
(There was a man)
Who had a goat
(Who had a goat)*

*He loved that goat
Indeed he did
He loved that goat
Just like a kid*

*One day that goat
Felt frisky and fine
Ate three red shirts
Right off the line
The man, he grabbed
Him by the back
And tied him to
A railroad track
Now, when that train
Heaved into sight
That goat grew pale
And green with fright
He heaved a sigh
As if in pain
Coughed up those shirts
And flagged the train*

# 106. But the cat came back

*Joining in with the chorus makes children feel part of a joyful event, which is both energizing and calming!*

## What you need: nothing

## What to do:

Lead the children by reciting the verses in a rhythmic way and encouraging them to join in the chorus.

*Old Mister Johnson had troubles of his own.*
*He had a yellow cat which wouldn't leave its home;*
*He tried and he tried to give the cat away.*
*He gave it to a man going far, far away.*

**But the cat came back the very next day.**
**The cat came back. We thought he was a goner,**
**But the cat came back, It just couldn't stay away.**
**Away, away, yea, yea, yea.**

*He gave it to a man going up in a balloon,*
*He told him for to take it to the man in the moon;*
*The balloon came down about ninety miles away,*
*Where he is now, well I dare not say.*

***chorus***

*He gave it to a man going way out West,*
*Told him for to take it to the one he loved the best;*
*First the train hit the curve, then it jumped the rail,*
*Not a soul was left behind to tell the gruesome tale.*

*Away across the ocean they did send the cat at last,*
*Vessel only out a day and making water fast;*
*People all began to pray, the boat began to toss,*
*A great big gust of wind came by and every soul was lost.*

*On a telegraph wire, sparrows sitting in a bunch,*
*The cat was feeling hungry, thought she'd like 'em for a lunch;*
*Climbing softly up the pole, and when she reached the top,*
*Put her foot upon the electric wire, which tied her in a knot.*

# 107. Different outcomes

*Helps the group to investigate ways in which to deal with problems calmly.*

## What you need: classroom storybooks

## What to do:

Choose a situation from a storybook and discuss each character's reaction and behaviour. Ask the children to talk about the outcome of her behaviour. For instance, you could read the story of Dick Whittington and discuss how he achieves success through clear thinking and dogged hard work.

Then ask them to retell the story by choosing an alternative response and thinking through how this would change the rest of the story. How could a different outcome be achieved?

Make sure that the group understands that the changed outcome is achieved through a change in the character's behaviour.

Try this with different stories. Ask the group to select stories they have enjoyed and use these to investigate how one change of behaviour could alter the whole chain of events of the rest of the story.

# 108. Pretend bedtime story

*This is a lovely, snugly way to calm everyone down.*

## What you need: a suitable story

## What to do:

Tell the group that you are all going to have a lovely little rest.

Turn off the lights.

Shut the blinds.

Ask the group to put their head in their arms and rest on the table.

Read them a bedtime story.

Now ask them to yawn and stretch and join in a group finger wiggle that will wake everyone up.

# 109. Send a ripple

*This calmer is a quick, cheerful mood leveller.*

## What you need: nothing

## What to do:

Explain that you are the rain, denoted by waving fingers. Each child must pass the action on around the class. Now become the thunder and mime this by slapping your knees. Again, the action should be passed from child to child. Finally, 'bring out the sun' by folding your arms and make sure this action is also passed around the group.

# 110. Cool in the hot seat

*This activity is a question and answer session on the theme of calm.*

## What you need: nothing

## What to do:

Choose a character or person who is a good example of calmness – sportsman, mythical hero, fireman/policeman, actor, etc.

Sit on a chair in front of the group. This chair is the 'hot seat'.

Introduce yourself as the person you are pretending to be for the duration of the hot seat.

Encourage the group to interview you in order to discover the secret of your calmness. For example:

> Leader: *Hello everybody, this afternoon I am going to be a gladiator. Who would like to ask me a question about how I keep my cool at the Roman Games?*
>
> Child 1: *How do you keep your cool before you go out into the arena?*
>
> Leader: *That's a good question. I have trained myself to stay calm by repeating over and over again, "I am strong and fearless. I am strong and fearless." Staying positive works for me.*
>
> Child 2: *How do you feel when you hear the crowd shouting and yelling at you?*
>
> Leader: *I focus on what I have to do. It took a bit of practise but I've learned to zone out distractions. Now I don't hear the crowd, I just concentrate on what I have to do. That keeps me clear-headed and calm.*

etc.

# 111. I'm a character, get me out of here

*This interesting activity encourages children to share calm, problem-solving skills.*

## What you need: space; story books

## What to do:

Ask each child to think of a story book character. Then they need to either use a situation from the story or to create a new one for their character.

Each child, in turn, is invited into the space where they introduce themselves and describe their problem or dilemma. Like this:

> *Hello, I'm Humpty Dumpty and I'm stuck on this wall.*
> *Get me out of here!*
> *Or,*
> *Hi, I'm Spider Man and I'm trapped in the cellar.*
> *Get me out of here.*

Then, using calm reasoning skills, volunteers can act out the character's rescue.
Ask the group to think of real-life situations that require calm thinking skills and act these out in the same way.

You may need to stress the importance of using calm, reasoned thinking. If any children make 'uncalm' suggestions, point out that these will make the situation worse or create more problems for the character.

Help children to evaluate their suggestions by asking questions like:

> *What would happen if the character chose that course of action?*
> *Who agrees that the character is staying calm and thinking carefully?*
> *Do we think that the character is thinking hard and staying calm?*
> *Does anyone have a better suggestion that would help the character?*

# 112. Floppy dolly

*An unusual way to teach relaxation to younger children.*

## What you need: a big, floppy doll or puppet; space; suitable music

## What to do:

Ask the group to sit in a space facing you.

Sit the floppy doll down and ask the children to copy how she sits.

Lift the doll to a floppy standing position and ask the group to imitate her.

Wiggle the doll around so that she dances in her special, floppy way and ask everyone to copy her movements.

Encourage the children to create their own floppy dolly dances.

# 113. Hand jive

*This activity will help children learn how to calm themselves.*

## What you need: calming music; examples of sign language or rock-and-roll hand jive

## What to do:

Show the children some examples of how we use our hands to communicate and respond to music. Ask them to show suitable (not rude!) hand signals that they already use.

Play calm music and ask them to concentrate on the hand movements that the music inspires. These will be strong, slow movements like rocking a baby or copying the movement of waves.

Ask them to create a series of calming hand movements and teach them to the rest of the group.

# 114. Snowflakes

*This calmer is a quiet game that everyone can play.*

## What you need: space

## What to do:

Everyone joins hands in a circle except for one child who stands in the middle. He/she is the snowflake.

The children move slowly round the circle chanting

> *Snowflakes floating,*
> *Snowflakes floating,*
> *Softly, softly,*
> *Hush, hush,*
> *Shhh, shhhhh.*

At the sound of, *shhh, shhhh*, the snowflake does a gentle, snowflake dance that everyone must copy.

The snowflake then changes places with a child in the circle and the chant begins again.

**Tip:** You can vary the game by choosing other floating things like boats, blossom or clouds.

# 115. Wind-up robot

*This calmer is a steadying activity for when things get too boisterous.*

## What you need: space

## What to do:

Tell the group that we all get 'wound up' sometimes and need to 'wind down'.

Put the group into pairs.

Ask the children to pretend that they have a big wind-up key on their backs.

Ask them to plan a dance that has four parts.

First they must wind each other up by turning the very heavy key on their partner's back.

Then they must move in a jerky, mechanical way, like a robot.

Gradually their movements slow as the key winds down. As they wind down they will become less rigid and more floppy.

Finally, they will move more slowly, flopping lower and lower until they are lying on the floor, very still and calm.

# 116. Cross cat, calm cat

*This activity helps children to investigate how we use our whole body to express emotion.*

## What you need: floor space; a wand

## What to do:

Choose a child to be a wizard and hold the magic wand.

Ask the wizard to go round the group and touch two or three children with his magic wand. He pretends to change the child into a cat.

He/she then gives instructions about how the 'cat' must behave:

> *Cuddly calm cat*
> *Angry cat*
> *Sleepy calm cat*
> *Wild cat*
> *Hunting cat*

etc.

The chosen children then act appropriately.

When the wizard says the word, stop, and taps the floor with his wand, all the cats must go back to their seats and other 'cats' are chosen.

# 117. Mirror, mirror

*Relaxation and concentration come together to make this a refreshing activity.*

## What you need: space; peaceful music

## What to do:

Put the children in pairs, facing one another.

Choose one to be leader and the other to be mirror.

Play gentle music and point out that their movements will need to be slow and gentle.

Allow everyone to develop their slow, calm, mirror dances.

After a while, the children can change roles, the mirror becoming the leader.

# 118. Sleeping lions

*This calming party game can be used to good effect in your setting.*

## What you need: space

## What to do:

Ask everyone to lie down on the floor like lions that are sleeping soundly.

The lions must not move in any way. Even if their tails twitch they will have to wake up and leave the game.

When a lion moves, you quietly tell them to leave the game.

The last child to move is the winner.

**Tip:** You can play this game as sleeping princesses or sleeping ghosts if you prefer.

# 119. Fill the space

*This is a quiet activity that requires slow movement and concentration and is suitable for older children.*

## What you need: space

## What to do:

Put the children face-to-face, in pairs.

Explain that when one child moves, the other must 'fill the space' by making the opposite movement. All movements must be slow and controlled. Like this:

One child crouches down – the other must stretch upward.

One child lifts their arms forward – the other must move theirs backwards.

One child leans to the right – the other leans to the left,

etc.

Develop these movements into a controlled sequence. Practise them and display to the rest of the group.

# 120. Act calm

*This activity shows children putting on a show of looking calm which is actually very calming!*

## What you need: space

## What to do:

Give the group some scenarios which require calm – playing a game, meeting a spaceship full of aliens, talking to a dragon, visiting the dentist, etc.

Act out playlets that demonstrate how calmness 'looks'. Talk about the visible signs (such as thinking hard, breathing slowly and steadily, taking time, relaxing their body).

Focus on these and ask the group, one by one, to show you what calm looks like.

**Tip:** You can remind the group of the behaviour of calm whenever they approach a stressful situation.